# Poetic Shades of Life 3

## Mr. Bad

Order this book online at www.trafford.com
or email orders@trafford.com

Most Trafford titles are also available at major online book retailers.

Printed in the United States of America.

ISBN: 978-1-4907-1332-8 (sc)
ISBN: 978-1-4907-1333-5 (e)

Trafford rev. 09/26/2013

 www.trafford.com

North America & international
toll-free: 1 888 232 4444 (USA & Canada)
fax: 812 355 4082

# TABLE OF CONTENTS

# INTRODUCTION

First, I would like to dedicate all the poems in this book to the people involved in the story who have made this book possible. This is the third and, hopefully, final edition that will tell of the strangest happenings and behaviors of the ones who are written about in this edition. The sequence of events, which have taken place in this book are mainly from the things and people I have heard, but never having actually seen or caught in the act. To the best of my knowledge, as I believe in my own actions and the things I hear, the events are actual, real, and are written about.

The previous times in the life of mine was that I grew up in the north side of my hometown, which was and is now even more the side of town that was and is trouble and most people either didn't go there or tried to get out. I grew up in a middle-class family with a total of six children born from my mother's womb. I was my mother's favorite and the most intelligent among the three sisters and two brothers I matured with. I advanced through elementary school, after head start and kindergarten, being the top grade student, with the exception of maybe one long dark haired very attractive girl who was very intelligent, but when it came to math I just seemed to be the quickest with the answers and I even took part in the fifth grade math class, during my fourth grade math class time. I then advanced into a high school in my hometown that expected a grade of B average or higher to be accepted into.

My career choice for learning there was mainly welding and technical drafting classes, along with machinist training. It was then in my sophomore year of classes that I started to get involved with hard drugs and by the time I was a junior in school, sleeping a class session away on the desk and dropping grades, showed me that the neighborhood started to get the best of me and I dropped out of school, before I received my diploma. I then started to get involved with all sorts of drugs with an ex-girlfriend of mine, whose name is tattooed on the outside of my right bicep under a rose that is pierced with a dagger.

The two years after I was sixteen seemed to be for me the worst in life, so I told myself enough was enough and went to test for the Armed Services. After a couple attempts, once trying to read the bleary questions and even being given a book with the questions and answers, I then finally got my eye-sight straight and passed for the United States Army, where my field of training was air defense artillery, as an electronics mechanic with missiles and launchers. I was happy with the employment, spending three years in Germany and receiving certificates to be one of the best in my field, among those soldiers who tested beside me.

Then it came, after a couple of girl-friends that I met a German girl who became my wife for eighteen years, giving birth to three children, which consisted of two daughters and a son. As a family we shared many good times and traveled throughout Europe on vacations, as I worked twelve years in a paper recycling plant there. I had smoked marijuana and hash the whole time through and like many, I also got drunk at many parties. Then, once again I met with the hard drugs and I started working high on speed and hardly sleeping or eating and I was put on medication because my behavior seemed not to fit other peoples' needs. The medication was strong enough to put a person in a chair after just ten minutes and interfered with my capabilities to work. I then stayed on medication, lamed and not being able to work for a five years, making attempts in-between to return to work, but was not able to handle the stress, as I was classified fifty percent handicapped.

Then I had a divorce and I lost of my only son who they say had taken his own life with a mix of liquid and tablets. I then spent a very lonely time in an apartment by myself and still I smoked hash and did other drugs with friends, as I was on medication and lonely. The need then led to my advancement away from the medication and I returned once again in the month of May in year 2000 to my hometown. I then started my life once again working full time and overtime without any problems at two fast food restaurants simultaneously while I attended the university in my hometown, as a full time student. At times I even worked sixty hours a week and studied full time with passing grades. I started then with Crack, a cooked Cocaine substance, which is smoked and it sure woke me up. The poetry then started as I wondered upon the voices and actions of others, as it then became apparent to me that I was being followed. I smoked openly and I knew I was being watched, but was not about to give up no freedom but instead put it all in the lines of the poetry, which is contained in "Poetic Shades of Life 1, 2, and Poetic Shades of Life-The Final Scripts."

It seems, as the story unfolded, that while I was working at a temporary labor service and making an attempt to get married with one of the two ladies I was pursuing and wrote about, a Japanese woman and a young blonde, that after I placed a phone call to a family member in Germany with the complaint that I was depressed and using drugs in the apartment complex where I was sharing or better said, given space for rent from another male individual, I noticed that the family member came to my hometown. So, the time went on and so did the poetry with my thoughts of what was happening on the side of secrecy, which seemed to be individuals following me and hiding in all places. I was being shadowed and my complaint moved from this family member who was now in my hometown stalking me to the detective's office and the Federal Bureau of Investigation. They all followed and there were many, as I jumped from job to job and also was suspended from school, due to failing grades and mental stress, trying to figure out what was happening and exactly who it was.

It seemed that the family member made an attempt to keep all women, girls, ladies, and such from me. This family member must have told them horror stories of the great monster I was and according to this family member I was even given the name, crazy, at that. This family member then got involved with Arabians, for whom I worked, with their unappreciated business ethics. There must have been some attempt at conspiracy against me because I had plenty of paperwork and mailings stating that I was winning money from sweepstakes and lotteries that I entered for six years with a total in entries and prize value at this point in June 2006 of 40,000 plus entries and with a total value of approximately $341,000,000.00.

The professionals, those from the university and the detectives, along with former employers had said that I was physically and mentally stable and in good health. I now, as I imagine, have lost the Japanese female who was sweet and polite because my daughter who in desperation refused to see the light and ran around with the Japanese woman, keeping her from me and telling many tales of falsification about me and also getting her molested from an Arab individual, Mo. The young blonde girl, who is now believed to be at this point seventeen and following me twenty-four hours a day seven days a week, wherever I go, seems to have had a baby-sitter, another Arab male, for whom I also worked who had been shot by her father because he sexually molested her in a bathroom in the night, as he was to guard her, as she stayed nights outside my house asking her father, who now is in prison for this, for entrance rights into my house. She also, then had an argument with her mother about me and after getting beaten and slapped, she killed her own mother in retaliation, and it is believed by me that the drugs they were giving her had an influence on her actions.

I am now in the possession of six written books, which could possibly be six compact poetry disks. I also have created a music cd with a wedding song I call Love Boat Alley and other dance songs for the world market, after I am married and having used it for my own wedding. One book I have written in German, which is titled Geschichte aus einem Leben (Story from a Life) and also contains stories about these sequences of events that have haunted me for two and a half years now. Currently, a major actress and model has also entered the scene in search of love and money. I now face the point, after having my daughter get pregnant and having a child, or not, the choice of three ladies, a Japanese woman, an actress, and the young blonde. I also await a line-up from people with my lottery wins or the truth that they are frauds from around the world, which in my calculation is $50,000,000.00 to $100,000,000.00. May God bless us all and grant serenity but give me the right choice, Amen.

# RUN FROM THE REAL

Something starts to distract me.
I hear it and it just may be.
I search for it to see.
I find nothing, but it must be.

I ask others, to hear what they know.
They say it must be the wind with a blow.
I heard it I say and it is so.
I know it is true and in my brain it has a glow.

"It is not there and not so", they say.
I wait and listen one more day.
I hear it I say, even when I lay.
"I don't know or think so", they say, but it may.

Many voices with plans that fit.
I listen and say, it is it.
I wonder, if I still have my wit.
It's real I say and with a loud hit.

Maybe so or maybe no.
Run I say and go.
Run from it to see, if it is so.
Run, run from the real and go.

3-07-06                                        Mr. Bad

This poem is written to express the fact that I know I am being followed and the people know it is true, but will not tell. I hear the voices from people who talk about me outside my house and everywhere I go. I must say that it has not been very amusing, especially when people will lie to me, trying to make me crazy as they protect my daughter who is following behind me. I started to hitch-hike once already, but returned as I was running from what was real, as everything was lied about to me. This poem is therefore titled "RUN FROM THE REAL."

# FOLLOW THE YELLOW BRICK ROAD!

From T-Town to life's future.
Long and narrow, but always the same color.
I'm on it, escaping the past's torture.
It's laid alright and with many a dollar.

Follow it, follow the yellow brick road!
When you get there you will find your gold.
Follow the yellow brick road!
Don't look left and right, it's all sold.

The dreams, adventures, and the trickery.
Yellow, yellow, till the end of time.
Follow the yellow brickery!
Sing, skip, and tell a rhyme.

Follow it, follow the yellow brick road!
Oz will be waiting at the end I'm told!
Follow the yellow brick road!
You'll have wishes three fold!

A long path indeed, they say.
A long yellow way.
Follow it, follow the yellow brick road!
Yellow, yellow, day after day.

3-14-06                                   Mr. Bad

Mr. Bad

This poem titled "FOLLOW THE YELLOW BRICK ROAD!" I wrote to express that I walk a path, like the yellow brick road in the film The Wizard of Oz. I attempt to better my life by writing books and playing music, but everyday seems as if I am walking down a long yellow road, trying to reach the Wizard and arrive to where I am trying to go. Life can be very difficult at times and a few more steps may be needed to reach a destination on this road.

# GEM

Shiny blue-eyed with the attractions.
The force pulls me in all directions.
Wittingly she comes with magnifications.
The view of her gives me satisfaction.

She quietly sneaks to search for probabilities.
The necessity is for abilities.
Her movements are of agilities.
The respects for her are hospitalities.

She glimmers with heavenly light.
Her curves are just right.
She could nibble and give the best bite.
I'm sure she would be the delight.

My temptation for her is a thrill.
My need for her is so real.
She sends chills through me with a wonderful feel.
The fruit of choice would have her peel.

From head to toe she shines like gold.
I have noticed that she is very bold.
I would hang a sign that says, I am sold.
Never should she turn me cold.

3-18-06                                    Mr. Bad

"GEM" is a poem written about a woman with shiny blue eyes and expresses how she makes me feel. She is a beautiful woman who had attracted me and she is known by many in the modeling and show business world. I feel as though she has come into my life and put a thrill into me. The poem is titled Gem because she was like a gem to me, so pretty and sparkly right. Even though, there is still one other who has been and is before her. A young blonde who I have asked to marry. One who is also written about in many of my other poems that I have written. So, this poem I had written as a tease to the Hollywood woman who decided to follow me in secrecy.

# BLUE SPARKLE

She has the shine and it shows in her eyes.
If I could, I would take away all her cries.
She has the words and you can hear them from her lips.
If I could, I would share all her sips.

She has the smell and she uses her nose.
If I could, I would give her a dose.
She has terrific hair with a brilliant flair.
If I could, I would comb it with care.

She has the ears and they are shaped so dear.
If I could, I would tell her not to fear.
She has the personality and it is audible when she talks.
If I could, I would tell her that she is like hawks.

She has the grooves and you can see it when she walks.
If I could, I would tell her she has balks.
She has the weapons and it shows with her guns.
If I could, I would say she ranks with her buns.

She has feet that lead a very nice path.
If I could, I would take away all her wrath.
She has it all and it shows.
If I could, I would tell her that she flows.

3-30-06                                        Mr. Bad

This poem "BLUE SPARKLE" is another poem which expresses how thrilling and respectful a certain woman is to me. The title Blue Sparkle is because she has sparkling blue eyes, which just seem to thrill me so much. I am in search of a woman and she may even be a class above me, but you never know how things may end in life. She is well known and very attractive to me, even though I feel lesser in value compared to her.

# DARK SKY

The lands start to rattle and shake.
The most inner core starts to bake.
The waters boil and waves roar.
The destruction starts at the core.

The lava encloses man and his kind.
The heat turns everything blind.
The future begins to dwindle.
The materials of life are in a thimble.

The sun's light turns three fold.
The heaven grows dark and cold.
The air becomes intoxicated with fumes from burning.
The people of the earth are yearning.

The light of life turns dark of death.
The valleys fill like a scorching heath.
The screams echo, as they rise.
The atmosphere is filled with cries.

The silence begins and all is still.
The spirit of life is halted once again, until.
The remembrance is faded and no thoughts are there.
The things we dear are all filled with fear.

3-31-06                                         Mr. Bad

Mr. Bad

"DARK SKY" is a poem written to express how the end of the world may be, if it comes with the crack through the planet earth, as has been told of. The lava, which will probably run out of the earth's core would most probably create a fire that would end life. Life as we know it would definitely end for a long time once again. This is a very scary situation, if there really is a crack that passes through the planet earth.

# TWO HEARTS

Like drums they beat with rhythm and soul.
They have the music of Noel.
Filled with the fluid of life, they pump.
They get louder and louder with each bump.

Two hearts and they thump and jump until they are one.
They are fulfilled with care, which weighs to a ton.
Singing and yearning for the other, they cry out.
They are two of a kind, headed on the same route.

Two hearts that are burning like wild fires, they rage.
They are free and can never be in a cage.
Like magnets, they are attracted to one another.
They have the power and can never smother.

Two hearts, like twins, one the same as the other.
They have faith and love, like a small child for its mother.
Swollen with love, they shimmer and glow.
They provide for the other and they flow.

Two hearts, which share the feelings and give life forever.
They stick together forever and they separate never.
Transformed into one, they join forces to heat.
Two hearts that together create the best beat.

4-5-06                                          Mr. Bad

"TWO HEARTS" is a poem, which expresses how it is when two individuals with their love for one another come together to be as one. It is a very special thing in life when two people are able to share their love with each other and have that special binding, which allows each person to grow and glow as life progresses. Love is a powerful tool, which can help people heal many grievances that they may have with themselves. Life can have many good and rough times, which come with it and hearts are the tools that can surpass through anything, if given proper care from the other.

# "CRACK"

It is snowy white, however, not as soft as snow.
It's not for the brave but for those who know.
It's cooked with care and treated by many as gold.
It can be bought, but it's mostly sold.

Some enjoy it and others may hate it more than all.
It can be found in the summer, spring, winter, and even in the fall.
It is something, that when tried, may start to call.
It can be rolled at times like a ball.

Snap, crackle, and pop it goes when you light it up.
When you have finished, it could make you feel like a pup.
The timing can be very short, until you feel like you're on top.
It makes some people jump, skip, run, and hop.

The name of it is for some first on their list.
For others there may always be a fist.
If used properly it could cure any depressive state.
For others, it could be their fate.

It has moved from place to place.
Some call it, first base.
At times it could be the fastest race.
Crack does have for some the greatest pace.

4-06-06                                          Mr. Bad

# Mr. Bad

This poem "CRACK" is written to express just how crack cocaine is for some people great and for others the worst thing in the world. I myself have smoked it and I have quit it. For me it was not such a bad thing, but there was talk about me as though I was the worst person in the world, which was not true. It just so happened that I myself had smoked crack and attended a university for three years, wrote several books, and produced enough music for two music compact disks on an organ. Things are not always what people may say, but instead they are what people make of them. In this instance crack cocaine. I would not recommend it to anyone but I would say that for me it helped to prosper and heal.

# POP TART THIEF

Morning, afternoon, or just a night's delight.
Pop tarts that taste just right.
Strawberry, chocolate, and there is especially a vanilla one outside my house.
Delicious indeed and they taste much better than any mouse.

Mickey the mouse is one who wants to bite.
He terrorizes my pop tarts every night.
Chocolate is available, but he really wants the vanilla one.
If he gets caught chewing, he will be done.

A pop tart terrorist and the pop tarts are in danger.
I warned them all, even the ranger.
Pop tart terrorist, Mickey, one with a hard head.
He really should stay home in bed.

The pop tart thief who wants to steal in the night.
The pop tart girls tell him that he is not alright.
The vanilla pop tart seems to be the one he likes best.
I keep telling him that he can steal the rest.

Pop tarts they may be and the best flavors.
I keep saying that nobody gets one with waivers.
The pop tart thief keeps trying.
The saying goes, that, here is no buying.

4-07-06                                             Mr. Bad

Mr. Bad

This is a poem written to express how others, especially one male, try to swing my women, one of whom I make an attempt to wed in matrimony, to his possession. There are two women, Japanese at the age of approximately thirty and an American girl of the age of 17 who follow me around to just about every place I go, along with my oldest daughter who also follows me and is twenty-five years old. As these women and my daughter follow me home and stand outside my rented three bedroom house, which stands in an area of business and being the only house around, they are hosted by a Palestinian or Mexican male, whichever he says he is and he attempted to swing my young blonde to drugs and sexually molest the young blonde or vanilla pop tart away from me and to him. His name is, Mickey, and he almost lost his life as he attempted to rape the young blonde who loves me so much.

The pop tarts are the three females, being Japanese, which is the chocolate with black hair, the young blonde American girl who is the vanilla pop tart with blonde hair, and the strawberry pop tart being my daughter who had red hair the last time I saw her. The pop tart thief being this Palestinian or Mexican male, whichever country he really comes from, who will not stay home and mind his own business, stalks the girls and me at my house constantly and causes many problems. I am aware of this because I hear them talk, fight, and argue. This poem is therefore titled "POP TART THIEF."

# TEASE

She said she will, as they steal my time.
Mostly, she waits for my dime.
There were those who wanted to choose.
There were those with boos.

I planted seeds and watched them grow.
I waited and now it has a flow.
The women wanted to help me with my rhymes.
Mostly, they wasted too many of the precious times.

The women have sneezed and teased.
I just wanted to breed.
They made me think they would come.
I'm still feeling so dumb.

The women say they love me and will share.
Still I wait to touch one hair.
There are others who receive that of mine.
I mark them with at least a nine.

They tease and I await the life.
They hurt me, as with a knife.
The time has come for me to maybe part.
They are like a sweet tart.

4-15-06                                             Mr. Bad

Mr. Bad

This is a poem I titled "TEASE" to reflect how I feel about the two women, of which only one I may wed. They seem to tell others that they are interested in me but leave me waiting like a tease. They both know that I am serious and mature and without a doubt I also care so dear. They have touched me both so deeply, but I receive not even a hello from either of them. To spill my heart out seems to be something they joke about. For me it is not funny anymore and the women should decide if they will come to my door. The waiting game has been about two years now, as they chase around my house and ponder upon me, as I anguish for them to simply knock on the door. I am indeed in possession of monetary funds that have been kept from me and to share it with them seems to be something they don't understand. So, I wait and maybe I'll need to find another girl who will come into my heart.

# PSYCHOLOGICAL

It all started a couple of years back.
The talk was of many things and even crack.
I was forced to stop a lot of things and give slack.
My work, school, freedom, and my mentality has been put on a rack.

Things got really bad and ended with people's death.
The fight that I had to put up took all my breath.
I growled, snapped, bit, and showed my set of teeth.
I swam, as if I was in one large heath.

The voices with real people behind them played the game.
The story is one to write about, but I'll be not the same.
The chase behind me was to end my life and give me the blame.
I was only looking to receive a dame.

There was a passionate love for me from one of none.
It was known by all, but not me, the one.
The search from me was for a wife and a son.
It shall be ended because I am done.

A daughter who tried to mark me and disturb my head.
Times of love and hate I have had, along with those times with no bread.
Dr. Jeckle, Mr. Hide and I started to call myself Sir Ed.
I really wonder, if there is something I must embed.

4-18-06                                             Mr. Bad

# Mr. Bad

This is a poem I have written and it has a story behind it. The story is that I have been titled or stereo typed, as a Crack-head from a daughter of mine with her Arab friend. This Arab immigrant has preyed upon her and the women who I have tried to be married to. From the two women, of which one was Japanese and the other a young blonde American, there has been plenty of controversy about me. The Japanese woman who I originally wanted to marry has hung on the side of my oldest daughter who has stalked me for a couple of years now. The young American girl has had, from what I have gathered, a love so great for me that plenty of controversy had risen.

There also was one Palestinian or Mexican man, whichever he rather titles himself, who has played as a babysitter outside my house, as the young American girl refused to be far from me and in love with me, as she attempted to rid me of my raped stalking daughter who had been raped or molested by a Jordanian man. Evidently, the Palestinian or Mexican man was shot by the young blonde girl's father in retaliation because he pushed his way on her in a bathroom, as she tried to use it by herself, which then led to her father going to prison, after shooting him.

An argument then arose between the young girl and her mother about me, which then for some reason had led to her mother's tragic death. I have had others outside my house the night of her mother's death and could actually hear it all taking place some miles away. The poem is, therefore, titled "PSYCHOLOGICAL" because it is evident to me what is being played, as everything seemed to be hidden from me.

# MY LOVE FOR HER

My love for her is so immense.
The feelings for her can be felt from a distance.
The heart I have for her is so intense.
The care I give for her is just an instance.

My love for her is the greatest of all.
The thoughts of her are tremendously spoken.
The sight of her makes me call.
The times with her can never be broken.

My love for her is of a king's for a queen.
The future with her shall be everlasting.
The respect I have towards her, is that, which has never been seen.
The vibrations from her are never passing.

My love for her fill my mind, body, and soul.
The boldness from her is that of no other woman before.
My love for her is a heart of a whole.
The sacredness from her is that which makes me soar.

My love for her is of the greatest debate.
My love for her is that of a shipmate.
My love for her is something you cannot rate.
My love for her.

4-18-06                                            Mr. Bad

"MY LOVE FOR HER" is a poem written to express how I feel towards a certain young woman who I have plans to be married to and make happy, until the end of our lives and enjoy every minute of life with her. She is a very special woman to me and she engulfs me with love like wild-fires that rage across plains of brush and cannot be distinguished by anyone. She is a young woman who is some years younger than I am and she has a passionate love for me. We both have been at fights with others actions to understand the love we have and show how passionate a love can be. I wait to see what the future holds for us both and to hold her in my arms forever with all my love.

# ONE MORE NIGHT?

I pray for help, as days come and nights go.
I await the one who will knock on the door and they know.
I ponder upon who takes the steps with their toes.
I wonder how many more nights and when they come, how many rows?

From dusk to dawn the fight becomes increasingly outrageous.
Could it be that something is spreading and contagious?
I seem to be the one who is allegeous.
They creep, crawl, and clutter me with that, which is not gorgeous.

The days go by and the nights are frightening.
It gets quieter when it rains with more lightning.
The way has been made and the end is tightening.
I am the happiest when the night starts its whitening.

It is such a terror to wait the night through.
I feel punishment waiting for her, as if I were black and blue.
They keep hiding secrets, but there are those with a clue.
Some nights disappear and there are those with déjà vu.

The secrets kept from me have become the most frightful.
One more night, I await a sight full.
I pray, as I wait with the knowledge of a delightful.
Please, not another night, awaiting an eyeful.

4-20-06                                          Mr. Bad

# Mr. Bad

This poem "ONE MORE NIGHT?" was written because I have this certain girl, who is a disc-jockey for a local rock 'n' roll radio station and she wants to come and live with me, but she seems to be having difficulties with her father's agreement of her having a relationship with me. She actually hangs around the outside of my house night and day, following me whenever I go, awaiting the chance from her father to let her come to the door.

The situation is that she has no mother alive anymore and her father is in prison while she waits for me at the age of seventeen. Meanwhile, there are these Arabs or Palestinian and Jordanian males who try to influence her with drugs to their side. There seems to be some danger involved also and, therefore, I wonder if it is acceptable for her having to wait another night or day outside. For me it is very scary and I hope not to lose her, even if I must wait until my death.

# THE WIN

A million to one, so they say.
When you have it you're second to none in every way.
Numbers, balls, tickets, and the chance to change.
The win could put a person in a different range.

Some become it or others may not.
It would make a person really hot.
Mixed, turned, twisted, and played for one.
The win would bring the brightest sun.

The past, present, and then there will be the future to come.
A seldom experience for most, but maybe multiples for some.
A win, one which could change your whole life.
A win, one which could cut like a knife.

Time may come and time may go, until you have won.
Some people say, they are done.
Like a river, which would suddenly flow in the opposite direction.
The win, hopefully, one without a citation.

Some play and some win.
Some may still hold their tin.
The win, one of every person's dreams.
The win, one which could bring all the different creams.

4-28-06                                                    Mr. Bad

"THE WIN" is a poem written to say that a person's life could really be different, if he or she won in a lottery or contest and received at least one million dollars. The difference in life usually has a monetary stepping stone that could make a person different and that very quickly. I myself have been living a very low income life and have won, but received the funds not. Money is a key tool to success and happiness, if it can be received. The deficiency of it, however, can make an individual sad, lonely, and also depressed. To those who do win and receive their winnings I would just like to tip my hat. No matter what walk of life they may have.

# BLONDE AND BEAUTIFUL

Really blonde they say and she is the best of all!
I sit waiting for her call.
She's not too heavy or small and not too short or tall.
Blonde and beautiful, I'd love to meet her in the hall!

She prances and dances, as she follows me wherever I go.
I'm not definite, but I'm sure I know.
Blonde and beautiful and it is so.
I'm not the only one, but I sure can turn the dough.

She has me so in love, so deep inside.
They all know that it cannot be denied.
She is so beautiful that I could never hide.
She is to be mine and I shall abide.

So beautiful, so blonde, and she is the best of all!
I'd have her by me, even in a stall.
We both are waiting for the greatest ball.
Never could I let this blonde girl fall.

She is so close, but yet so far.
So blonde, so beautiful, and she can hold like tar.
I could imagine her in a sport car.
Blonde and beautiful she is and the prize of a czar.

4-30-06                                             Mr. Bad

This poem is written about a young blonde woman who has followed me for some time now. She is beautiful to me and she talks of care for me, as she follows me. I know this because I can clearly hear it night and day wherever I go. We both have not met but we are constantly so close together and yet she is kept distant from me, awaiting permission from her father to meet me. She has followed me now for approximately two years in secrecy, fighting against my oldest daughter who attempts evil upon me and also follows me in secrecy with stories of falsifications. I have titled this poem "BLONDE AND BEAUTIFUL" because from the pictures I have seen of her, she is exactly that.

# JUST YOU

There is no other who fills my heart with so much joy.
There is no other which I would say is my best toy.
There is no other and she is not a boy.
Just you and I do greatly enjoy.

Passing daylight and sleepless nights keep me waiting for you.
I could think of nothing, as much as I do you too.
There is not a thing that amuses me like you, not even a zoo.
Just you and I do.

Open skies and buried grounds could not stop the feel.
No person could have anything hidden like your special seal.
I could never be halted and I could wait forever until.
Just you and you are the best pill.

No secrets in the entire world could make me so curious.
Any barricades in my way to you would make me furious.
No girl as you do makes me so murderous.
Just you and I am serious.

So sugary sweet and fruitful to me.
I pray and wait that you'll be.
Just you, I want to see.
Just you and with creed.

5-01-06                                            Mr. Bad

Mr. Bad

This poem "JUST YOU" I have written for a girl who is in my heart and who is also written about in other poems and her name is, Sheri Vegas. She is a sweet young girl, who I have fallen in love with and someday would like to get married to her and have children with her. We have not personally met yet but she has been all the thoughts and prayers that I have. We have been through rough and sweet times together even though we have not met because her father has not allowed our acquaintance, but she follows me every step I take and we both know it.

# ROADSIDE

It's there, the roadside, for me and you.
We may walk it, jog it, and skip too.
I see it, the roadside, red, white, and blue.
If a person looks close enough there may be Sue.

Roadside, have you seen it too?
There is something that does not fit.
If something is needed, it may be there to get.
It seems to be built with a kit.

Sometimes it is pretty, but other times very sick.
There is something that you may check with a stick.
Pencils, crayons, papers, and perhaps a brick.
I wish I really could take a better pick.

Roadside that is filled with all that is deeded.
Mostly though, it is needed.
The main ingredients it has, as it is seeded.
I wonder why it is never weeded.

Wood, guns, money, bottles, cans, and such.
Roadside, it has even car parts and much.
So many things and indeed it needs a good touch.
Roadside, and people fill it as they push their clutch.

5-08-06                                            Mr. Bad

"ROADSIDE" is a poem written to express how filled with trash most city streets in my hometown are and most likely other city streets also. I myself at the moment do not drive, so I walk wherever I go and become a first-hand look at everything, which lies on the roadside. At times there are things that could be needed or used and I may pick those things up; such as money, straps for the boat or holiday vacations, tools, and much more. I have always wondered as I walk, which day there will not be a dead animal but a dead person. If you have the opportunity to read this poem give it a thought and a good look as you walk down the street the next time.

I have won money in sweepstakes and lotteries, which I know about, but have received none and even offered the mayor's office in my home town money to clean the streets and help the homeless, if I received mine, but this never happened because I was denied the money I won. It is a very terrible thing that the streets are not properly and on a regular basis cleaned. I myself am really tired of seeing all the trash on the roadside.

# HONESTY

When used it helps a person who may need.
It is a very powerful thing, but may seem like a tiny seed.
All people should use it with their creed.
Honesty should be every person's lead.

Most individuals should have it, but they do not.
If it is needed, give it your best shot.
Some express it and even end it with a dot.
The best is when you have got.

Honesty, the best thing a person can use.
It is not something to abuse.
Some pay with it and others receive their dues.
Honesty is something that would not confuse.

It is always helpful and makes others think twice.
The more the better and honesty is so nice.
If not needed, still peep it like a mouse.
Honesty honesty, even if it is as small as rice.

To receive it from others is a wonderful thing.
It will shine like, bling bling.
Honesty can give flight with the greatest wing.
Honesty is like wearing a halo that is a golden ring.

5-11-06

Mr. Bad

Mr. Bad

This is a poem written to express how important and great it is for people to be honest and it is titled "HONESTY." I have been confronted with enough dishonesty in the past several years and realize how important honesty is. Times may have reasons that honesty could be difficult to use but honesty should always come first hand. Honesty can create a much better picture for one's self than dishonesty anytime in life and in the eyes of God.

# COVER-UP

It's in the wind and I also hear it all.
They shout, holler, argue, talk, and call.
It's all hidden from me, the girls and the money.
If life could be sweet, this surely is no honey.

They hide outside my windows with their jealousy and grief.
They think I know nothing but I am in belief.
There seems to be something that I must not be told.
I talk and I shout out at them, as I am so bold.

FBI, CIA, Sheriff, Police, whichever I am hidden from.
I hear it be told to give him some.
Cover-up and they think I do not know.
They all may lie to me and say it is not so.

All day and all night I'm followed like a shadow from the dark.
Sooner or later I will give a very large spark.
The paperwork I have says it all and they do too.
I feel as though I must say boo.

There are many involved but I may not be aware.
Tricks are played and they try to scare.
Cover-up and with many voices, which say many things.
Crazy I am not and I do know when it rings.

5-12-06                                    Mr. Bad

This poem titled "COVER-UP" is a poem about me and all the strange happenings around me, as I fit all the puzzle's pieces together. It seems as though my oldest daughter came from Germany and has been following me around and telling people bad things about me. I heard her and others talking, as I was in an apartment complex doing homework for the university which I attended. It must have been said that I was using drugs and acting abnormal, which had brought my oldest daughter from Germany, who then had stalked me constantly, as she got involved with some Arabian males who I worked for at a carry-out store and gas station.

The effects of it all were that I had to quit going to classes at the university in my hometown, stop working at four different places of employment, and listen as they played games on the two women, of which I wanted to be married to. Time has passed now, approximately two years and the information and happenings are that my daughter has been using an excuse that I was crazy and on drugs to stop my winnings of millions that I won in lotteries and sweepstakes. The daughter involved had been accompanied by a female Japanese teacher of mine, as my daughter played her off me with lies and games while my daughter herself was raped or abused and became pregnant. The other woman, a young blonde American girl had also been following me and fighting for me and my winnings, against my daughter and the Japanese woman, who never did say hello. It has come to the fact that the detective's office was behind me as my daughter used her excuses against me to stop my winnings, which I had won.

The young blonde girl was raped or molested by one of the Arab men, who played guard for her as she spent nights outside my house. She then told her father of the abuse who then shot the man and spent time in prison. There was then another argument about me between the young blonde and her mother, as she was slapped several times by her mother and turned to retaliation and then killed her mother.

As this all happened, it seems that one of Hollywood's actresses also started to make plans with me. The blonde girl, however, has been my choice because of the actions she has taken and the sorrow, which accompanies whatever it may be that has created these awful events. She now must use the law and her grandfather to get the right to live with me because her father will not give his consent but makes her wait. She is at this time only seventeen and still follows me every step of the way.

Mr. Bad

# SOME DAY

We all want, wish, and pray.
There is always hope for the day.
Need is part of life and I also await the say.
Wait, wait, and wait but hopefully I will not decay.

From heaven to earth and beyond we search for something.
I have learned what it means to have nothing.
I'm also told I may have none because I did a different thing.
I'll strive though for anything.

Passionate love for another is for me on top of the list.
I fight amongst many and still shake at heaven my fist.
Jesus in heaven and God of us all must know that I'm amidst.
I'm looked upon and always I try to assist.

Time has gone and time has come, as I build.
I read what is before me, even on a shield.
I sit watching and waiting amongst those who have thrilled.
With a flowering space of many there could be only one in the field.

The stars twinkle and the sun shines.
Time passes, as I wait with these rhymes.
Life is filled with many different grimes.
Someday there may be the times.

5-15-06                                             Mr. Bad

"SOME DAY" is a poem to express how I await the day, as I sit lonely and far under the poverty level for a partner, actually a woman and daughter, along with some money to share time with me. I have for some time now stopped working or better said, work only what I must to survive because I have been stalked and put down to the point that I await for people to see what a great person I really am.

There is the young blonde girl who is seventeen years old and I have waited for her to share my wealth and fortune with me, which I build constantly by writing books and entering sweepstakes by the thousands and even creating music for our wedding day.

# THE CREATURES FROM THE DARK LAGOON

In the darkness they lurk and prey.
I hear them in the distance night and day.
They really do have a lot to say.
These creatures are everywhere, even at the bay.

From the depths of divinity they surely do come.
There are not just a few, but some.
They prey upon me, but I'm not dumb.
The total is of the sum.

Screeching and yearning, they attempt to hurt me.
With fangs of phantoms and wings of the Devil they try to be.
There can be only one hero and that we will see.
A name for them cannot be found but may start with a D.

They are heard, but not seen as they creep and crawl.
If asked, I wonder what I should draw.
I sense them everywhere, even in the wall.
I hear them scratch with a great claw.

Spook and sprawl as they attempt to decoy.
Many are there, these creatures who deploy.
The creatures of the dark want to destroy.

5-20-06                                             Mr. Bad

40

This poem "THE CREATURES FROM THE DARK LAGOON" was written about those who follow me. They have not been caught but they are clearly heard and surely there, everywhere around me and wherever I go. Three women have been following me and have drawn on many others, along with those creatures from the dark lagoon who want to destroy me and the things about me. If I had to think of a name for those or draw them, I would not know where to start because they are that bad.

# DAYS WASTED

The days begin, as my eye-lids rise.
The thoughts are of maybe a better way.
The feelings are that there will be more lies.
The start is for another day.
The probabilities for progress are most likely the cries.
The wish is for better, if I may.
The hope is that the deserving dies.
The necessity for life is what will say.
The progress of a day is with goodbyes.
The steps taken seem to be all on clay.
The need is for the prayers to arise.
The want seems to be so gay.
The prayer goes out to the one who flies.
The times of sadness seem not to decay.
The sounds are of her with other guys.
The dreams are from those who lay in hay.
The depression is given from the one who denies.
The scene comes, as that of the bay.
The sights are all written in the skies.
The days are wasted as I wait again for another nay.

5-22-06                                    Mr. Bad

This is a poem titled "DAYS WASTED" and is written because I feel as though my days are always being spent away, as I wait for a hello from the females who follow me everywhere I go. A daughter and two possible wives, along with an actress and my youngest daughter seem to be following me and they are being followed themselves from two Arabs who attempt to lie to me, as one of them attempts to mistreat my daughter and the other attempts to disrupt a building relationship, which I have been working towards with a young blonde female.

The wait has been some time now, as neither my daughters nor the females will say hello or let themselves be seen by me. I have had a dream of a better life for some time now, but as long as I am forced to loneliness the days are wasted.

Mr. Bad

# KILLER HIT

Killer this and killer that, what is with the real world?
Hit this and hit that, how many hits until it is right?
Ask this and ask that, what is really the curled?
See this and see that, but did I hear it in my sight?

They will or they will not, how long until the night?
She only leads the time of spot or not?
Push this and push that, where is the push that might?
Play this and play that, but what is really hot?

Hear this and hear that, did I hear anything at all?
Look at this and look at that, but is there someone I might see?
Answer this and answer that, but did one try to call?
Say this and say that, but will someone say to me?

Killer hit, killer hit, will it make me fit?
All was tried, but was one the rest?
Killer hit, killer hit, will it make me lit?
Hit it, hit it, until you're the best?

Apples, peaches, and Pumpkin died.
Killer took her from my side.
She hit killer and killer hit.
She killed the hit that hit the killer's kit.

05-25-06

Mr. Bad

"KILLER HIT" is a poem written because it seems that one of the girls who follows me has smoked crack, which is cocaine and seems to have found herself in a little trouble with those she gets it from. There is always plenty of talk about those who may smoke crack, but not all people are the same. Crack is a very lethal and problem causing drug, which has caused pain to many people in today's world.

# MEMORY LANE

It's a highway, which is constructed as we live our lives.
It's a fast and a slow lane without the division.
It's an ocean to live in and some try dives.
It's a book we open when we think of our decisions.

As time passes we all stop to read a page.
There is always a beginning, but never an end.
The stories we tell could be young or come with age.
We glance at times through the memories and maybe defend.

Some words may be bleary on memory lane.
The thoughts may be weary, as we retrace them again.
Some memories could be clear and filled with fear or maybe insane.
There are those we dislike most and those that give us daily estrogen.

Like stripes of a divided street, the memories pass as we progress
through miles.
There are also those lanes in which there is no separation.
There are those memories, which for some reach the Nile's.
The tracks we leave behind may even come from desperation.

Lane after lane we turn and change for the next.
The undergrowth upon which we walk memory lane is an abundance
of many different grains.
Memory lane can be talked about or put in text.
Some may draw it, some may construct it, and some may walk
memory lane without brains.

5-27-06                                    Mr. Bad

This is a poem that makes an attempt to express how our memories are like a road or path, which will create our ways with each day. Peoples' memories are very different or unique with each different life from which they are made, like different lanes of memories and is, therefore, titled "MEMORY LANE." At times we all stop to think of one memory or another and consider what we have enjoyed or disliked about each memory. Some memories are of love and life while others may derive from sadness or death. There are those memories which we repeatedly recall and others we never want to know at all. Memories are good things and the more the better ones, the better we have of life.

# MENTAL TERROR

First I started to wonder and then I listened.
Many voices I heard and they came from many different places.
Then I listened to see who was missing.
Many games played from different bases.

The ways I travel are shadowed by many.
They all come to watch, but would not talk.
They are the ones I know, not just any.
There were those who could not take a long walk.

Faith I kept for myself, as the others all lied.
I was told that there was no one.
I have been the only on my side.
There is a fact that I'm second to none.

They all follow, argue, complain, and defend.
The talk was loud and clear, so I prayed to depend.
I said I was right, even if I must spend.
I asked for an angel of reality that would mend.

A large amount of chaos and hate has been caused.
The terror is caught now and paused.
The truth of a daughter who tried to scam me is now true.
I ask now, above, can it be blue.

5-27-06                                            Mr. Bad

"MENTAL TERROR" was written because I have been mentally terrorized for some time now, as the terrorist believed I knew nothing. In search of a woman while being stalked from a daughter who joined forces with an Arab male to terrorize and put a scandal on me. I was terrorize and lied to. A daughter who had been brutally treated and helped Arabs to put shame and discrimination on me had been following me, trying to stop any money I might win with the 41,000 sweepstake and lottery entries I have. The talk has been clear about me and the money I did win, but received none and the terror upon me has led to much hate. Not only was I followed by a daughter but the daughter managed to keep all women away from me, as I make an attempt to get married once again.

# THE MEMORIAL WAY

Those who have fought for the ways.
Those brave ones who spent their days.
Those with their courage for freedom.
Those who have made certain things be done.

Those memories which are embedded in each of us.
Those memories that could fill more than a bus.
Those memories, those that are dreaded for time to come.
Those memories, which were made for some.

The pain, the torture, and the hate was dug in trenches.
The agony, the tears, and the memories of those on benches.
The prayers, the plea, and the scars of those in action.
The memories that are only a fraction.

The lives and the blood spilled stains us all forever.
The battle lines of many places are removed never.
The stories that are told are unimaginable for many.
The time spent is not just of others or any.

The memorial way is that which should not be forgotten.
The way of memorial is that which keeps on dotting.
The day of memorial shall stand for thanks.
The memories are for those who stood in ranks.

5-30-06                                            Mr. Bad

"THE MEMORIAL WAY" is a poem that on Memorial Day was written and to express the remembrance and thanks that shall be carried in the future forever for those who gave their lives for freedom and against terror, so that others may have a life of happiness. There is so much to be thankful for from those who did not share in the loss of blood and in the name of Liberty.

# TWO SNEAKS AND NO SHEIK

They watch like vultures in the sky.
They wait until their meal is just fine.
They listen to hear, if there is a cry.
They stalk for something to dine.

Two sneaks with their crooked beaks.
Day and night they lay out their bait.
Two sneaks and they are geeks.
Rain or shine, they fill their crate.

They attempt to overthrow my temple.
The need is for that which is mine.
Their need is for my stencil.
They try to fish with their tangled line.

Two sneaks and they reek.
The more they try the weaker they get.
No sheik, but there are two that sneak.
Two sneaks and no sheik and they do not quit.

Time will come when they will lose.
They have been warned too many times.
They will have to pay the highest dues.
Two sneaks and I write the rhymes.

6-5-06                                                    Mr. Bad

"TWO SNEAKS AND NO SHEIK" is a poem written and believed to have a true life story behind it. It is about one Palestinian male and a Jordanian male, of which one had tricked my daughter into causing me many troubles and another who tries to steal a young blonde girl from me, causing enough anger and heartache, as I attempt to be married to her and have children once again. I am forced to listen to them both, along with others, as I hear them stalking her, as she also follows me wherever I go. They are two sneaks who evidently do not follow the words of God very closely who would be the sheik.

# ALL ACES AND NO FACES

There are those who may play poker for fun.
Then there are the ones who play for a ton.
Some may last until the last card is done.
I receive all the aces and I'm the one.

We all shuffle, stack, cut, and deal to get the highest card.
Some may bet or try too hard.
The game of poker may take place inside or perhaps out in the yard.
Some play with hands that seem to be smeared with lard.

The game of poker has its rules too.
There are those who try to be you.
At times there are the ones who bluff and say boo.
I play with many and still I say, I do.

The hand which is best is the one with all the aces.
The hand I hold, which contains no faces.
Some may play with all they have and arrive with cases.
They might dress so fine or come without laces.

I play the game myself, but with a stacked deck.
The others may wonder how and say, heck.
They look very closely to see, if there is a fleck.
I play with those who have lost up to their neck.

6-08-06                                          Mr. Bad

This is a poem I have written to express that no matter what is played against me in my home town from the two Arabs and a Hollywood movie star who is trying to keep my, Sunshine Baby, a young blonde girl away from me, progress will happen. I feel that this game, which is being played, would be poker and is played by me with the best hand of aces. There are the others with what I call a mixed hand of face cards who cannot be honest and play fair to have me as a husband. I myself know what is played against me to stop the things I have been working towards and receive the girl who in my opinion is a young blooded blonde and be married once again.

I have been having a rough time, after passing the Japanese woman up and falling in love with a young blonde girl, as I have been sidetracked from a Hollywood actress and model named Jennifer. After entering over 40,000 sweepstakes and lotteries I also have heard of a bundle of cash I have won, which has been delayed by a daughter of mine who seems to have spread many lies about me, as she got herself involved with an Arab who has even beaten her at times. This poem is therefore titled "ALL ACES AND NO FACES."

# THE NON-EMERGENCY CALL

It was whispered that one had called.
Another came from the distance, but did not help at all.
A new life had been awaited, but then it was stalled.
I was climbing even higher and then I had to fall.

The talk from the distance about me proved to be wrong.
I achieved great stories for myself and even a song.
Many problems had risen from this call.
They say I did not see, but I saw.

Many people got involved from this call to the distant.
I recognized what was happening in an instant.
They played and pondered upon me to see what was right.
I challenged them all, as I put up a great fight.

A terrible deed had been put on my soul.
This one from the distance laughed, as I sat with my empty bowl.
Hatred has grown for this one from the distance.
The attempt was to make me an instance.

A great mistake had been called about me.
There were many who had come to see.
They watched in the darkness and in the light.
I heard them all say that I was right.

6-11-06                                    Mr. Bad

This poem titled "THE NON-EMERGENCY CALL" was written about the sequence of events, which I have been going through from the year 2003 to 2006. It seems that an emergency call brought my daughter from Germany to my hometown. She, however, upon her arrival never came to my doorstep or knocked on the door to see what the telephone call to her was actually about. It had been said that I was using drugs and shouting, as I sat alone in my apartment. My daughter who upon her arrival from Germany began to stalk me and she told others that I was insane, but this is not the case because I have even more education than she has herself. She apparently had gotten involved with some Arabs who attempted to lie to me and say that she was not in town, so that they could have their pleasures with her and even attempt to manipulate her into some very bad things.

I also had been stalked so badly that the only thing for me to do was to stop working, starve myself most of the time, and stop attending the university, which I was enrolled in, until I had received help from others to prove that she was indeed following me and trying to mark me as a bad individual.

# THE BANG!

A sweetheart's treasure or a robber's grin?
A long time has passed and the time has grown thin.
A banker's delight or a poor man's tin?
A time of sorrow and they say I've been.

A ping and a pang or a boom and a bang?
A wait, but it never rang.
A thing or a thang, did it have zang?
A wish of many or just a dang.

A decision of God or a saint's relief?
A story for many who deny, but I remain in belief.
A merchant's surprise or a dirty little thief?
A bundle of joy, but a brand new grief.

A lucky man's win or a dummy's luck?
A straight arrow's hit and a crisp buck.
A golfer's stroke or a new puck?
A delight for us all and a very tight tuck.

A chest full or a chip of a lot?
A sentence to sign and give a dot.
A dime or maybe a dollar, could it be the one I got?
A small package or a great big pot?

6-14-06

Mr. Bad

"THE BANG!" has been written, as I await a large sum of money, which I have won, but not received. A big change shall come, hopefully, and a big bang. I have lived sometime now, about three years at the moment, pretty much without money and awaiting my share from entering sweepstakes and lotteries on the Internet daily. There were many rumors about me, which should not hold me up. I have been halted from freedom and liberty, along with privacy of my life and this denies me the right, as other individuals to live. I'm hoping and praying that justice will be served out and I'll get my bang!

# THE BOOM!

D reams to become reality with lusters of gold.
I played and waited as I acted bold.
Truth which was hidden makes the future a thing.
I can't wait for the bling bling.

They threw traps and changed maps.
Still, I hit them with all the raps.
My mind is changing for a better start.
It is pierced, as with a dart.

There are those who choose for me.
I heard it all, but did not see.
They were asked and they said, "no."
It should be my turn now to row.

With chest to the best.
The tracks are led after the test.
They tried and they lied but the wish was too short.
The mystery was vast and one to abort.

Rumble and roar, it's time to pour.
I've been beaten, but I'm not sore.
The sound is tremendous and rages with more.
The Adam should be given from the core.

6-14-06                                   Mr. Bad

This poem "THE BOOM!" is a poem that tells of the attempt from certain individuals to stop my monetary progress in life. It expresses the fact that I will become money to do many things with; things I never thought would have been possible, such as buying a Porsche, paying cash for a house, getting married, and much more. There has been the attempt to put a marking on me, as an abnormal individual, which has already been proven to be false. I shall be married once again, receive the money that was not righteously kept from me and have children of which one will be another son. There have been certain people who have made false statements about me and also those who were jealous. Then there have been those who have come to say that I am normal and being falsely denied my rights to a better life.

Mr. Bad

# THE WORLD FOR HER!

Eagle eyes and with the legalize!
The best from stalk and soar like a hawk!
So fine, that heart is mine!
It will be the best dine!

She laughs and she giggles, then there is the wiggle!
She does it and she's not in the middle!
Like an illuminated freight-train she roars through!
She's there with the dawn and dew!

The nibble and the nab!
She has what I want to grab!
Shiny clean while she's sneaky mean!
She tops the list, she's the dean!

Chained like a dragon, but she pulls the greatest force!
My pick of all, she is the best horse!
Brilliant with flair, she is the one to know!
She has the greatest show!

The atmosphere is filled with presence of love!
I look with gratitude up above!
The whole world shakes for her!
She is to be for sure!

6-18-06                                    Mr. Bad

I have written this poem with a little flair to express how I really feel for a young girl who follows me, Sheri, and how I feel about her dedication to be with me and she seems to stop for nothing, as she waits to live with me. I feel as though God himself has sent this young girl to me and I am grateful for this, but first she must put up a great battle to receive the wedding with the wedding song I have created, along with the wealth which shall be built. It is therefore titled "THE WORLD FOR HER!"

# THE SCENERY

At times it is light and at times it is dark.
It may glow crimson green or be so white.
Silence seems to be, but in the distance is always the bark.
The audience denies their presence, but I hear the crowd's fight.

The scenery changes with every step and yet it remains the same.
There is always the empty visual, but the vocals fill the air.
I listen like a hunter, but can take no aim.
The background speaks, shouts, and cries with fright of a bear.

I listen with suspense, as I look for the show's next act.
The characters are staged with the presence of none.
The show is real, but without a fact.
At times there is laughter and fun.

There is plenty of fright and there are those who are right.
The scenery is still with the movements of the past.
The show starts with the morning bright and intensifies in the night.
There seems to be a great variety of cast.

The scenery changes, but yet remains the same.
The sounds come from trees and open pastures.
There are many and yet not one name.
Like seas and rivers, there are fish in raptures.

7-5-06                                                Mr. Bad

"THE SCENERY" is a poem written about me hearing individuals outside my house who follow me, to see what I am about. I listen, as there are arguments about me and money I have won, along with the jealousy of two males who don't like the fact that I have a young girlfriend who really loves me and wants to be my wife. There is a lot of talk and arguments, along with the jealousy, which takes place but still I wait for a change in life and to receive a girl who will come and live with me to be my wife.

# The End